Earth and the Sun

Bobbie Kalman and Kelley MacAulay

Crabtree Publishing Company
www.crabtreebooks.com

Created by Bobbie Kalman

For Julie and Joel Mercer
I love you both soooooo much!

Editor-in-Chief
Bobbie Kalman

Writing team
Bobbie Kalman
Kelley MacAulay

Editor
Robin Johnson

Copy editor
Michael Hodge

Photo research
Bobbie Kalman
Crystal Sikkens

Design
Katherine Berti
Samantha Crabtree (cover)

Production coordinator
Katherine Berti

Illustrations
Barbara Bedell: pages 17, 20
Katherine Berti: pages 10, 14, 15, 27

Photographs
© Dreamstime.com: page 5 (inset)
© iStockphoto.com: page 30 (bottom)
© Shutterstock.com: cover, pages 3, 4, 5 (except inset), 6, 7, 8, 9 (except top right), 10, 11, 12, 13, 16, 17, 18, 19, 20, 21, 22, 23, 24, 25, 26, 27, 28, 29, 30 (top), 31
Other images by Digital Stock

Library and Archives Canada Cataloguing in Publication

Kalman, Bobbie, 1947-
Earth and the sun / Bobbie Kalman & Kelley MacAulay.

(Looking at earth)
Includes index.
ISBN 978-0-7787-3202-0 (bound).--ISBN 978-0-7787-3212-9 (pbk.)

1. Sun--Juvenile literature. 2. Earth--Juvenile literature.
I. MacAulay, Kelley II. Title. III. Series.

QB521.5.K34 2008 j523.7 C2008-900925-8

Library of Congress Cataloging-in-Publication Data

Kalman, Bobbie.
Earth and the sun / Bobbie Kalman and Kelley MacAulay.
p. cm. -- (Looking at earth)
Includes index.
ISBN-13: 978-0-7787-3202-0 (rlb)
ISBN-10: 0-7787-3202-9 (rlb)
ISBN-13: 978-0-7787-3212-9 (pb)
ISBN-10: 0-7787-3212-6 (pb)
1. Sun--Juvenile literature. 2. Earth--Juvenile literature.
I. MacAulay, Kelley. II. Title.
QB521.5.K35 2008
523.7--dc22
2008004843

Crabtree Publishing Company

www.crabtreebooks.com 1-800-387-7650

Printed in the U.S.A./112014/CG20141104

Published in Canada
Crabtree Publishing
616 Welland Ave.
St. Catharines, Ontario
L2M 5V6

Published in the United States
Crabtree Publishing
PMB 59051
350 Fifth Avenue, 59th Floor
New York, New York 10118

Published in the United Kingdom
Crabtree Publishing
Maritime House
Basin Road North, Hove
BN41 1WR

Published in Australia
Crabtree Publishing
3 Charles Street
Coburg North
VIC, 3058

Contents

Earth and the sun

The sun shines light onto Earth. Without the sun's light, Earth would be very dark. The sun also heats Earth. Earth would be cold and frozen without the sun's heat. Without the sun's light and heat, there would be no life on Earth.

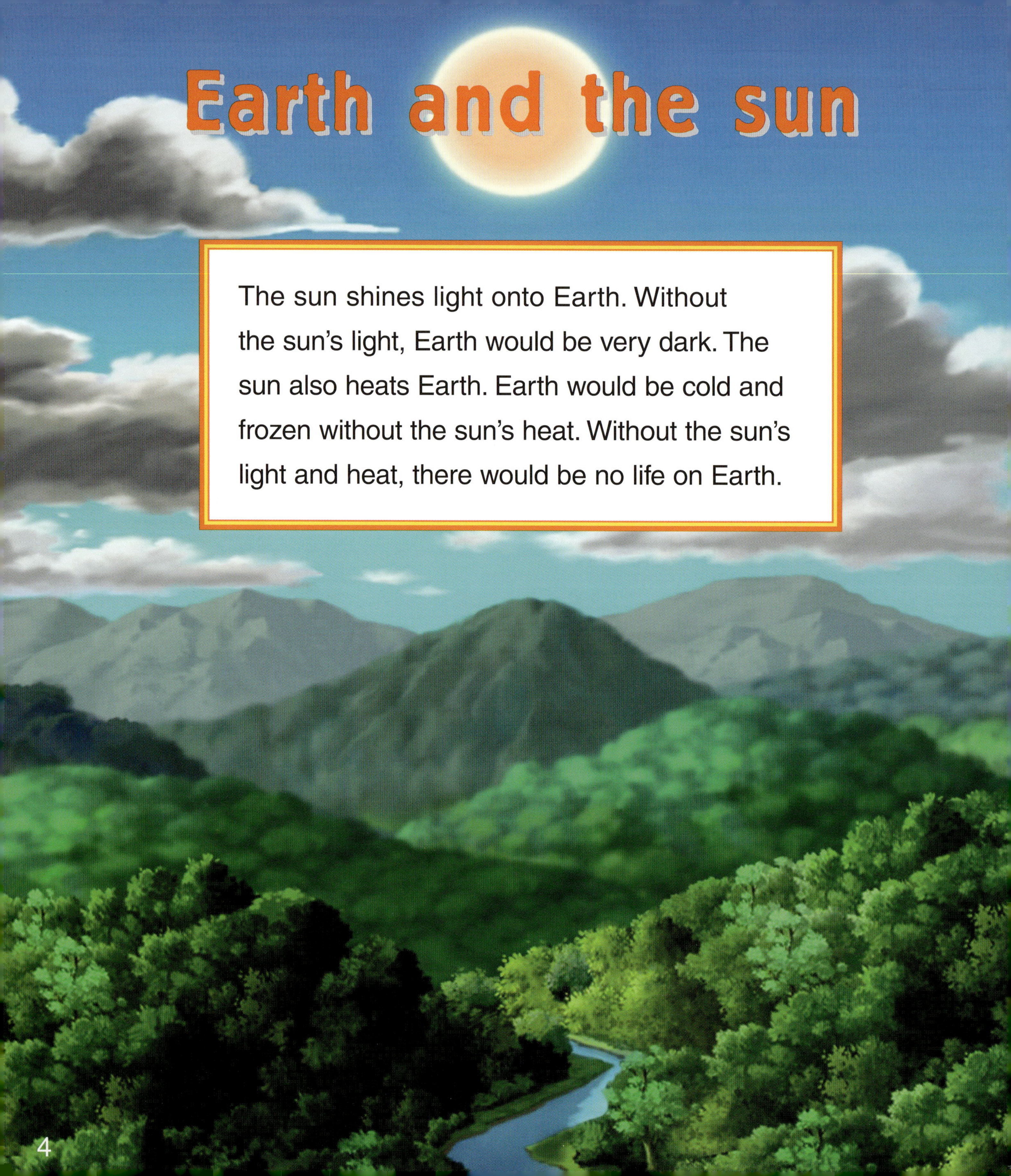

Gifts from the sun

We love sunny days! The sun warms us and makes us feel good. We love to see the beautiful colors of flowers. We love to swim on hot summer days. We love the food we eat. Did you know that the sun gives us all these gifts?

The sun gives us the foods we eat. It also gives us colors.

What is the sun?

The sun is a **star**. A star is a huge, hot ball of gas that glows and gives off heat. The sun is the closest star to Earth. It is still very far away, though! The sun is much bigger than Earth is, but it looks small because it is so far away.

The sun is a medium-sized star. Some stars are bigger than the sun. Others are much smaller. We see the stars as tiny white lights in the night sky.

The solar system

The sun is at the center of our **solar system**. The solar system is made up of the sun, **planets**, moons, and other things that float in space. The sun does not move. The planets **orbit**, or move in circles, around the sun. Earth is a planet. It is the third-closest planet to the sun.

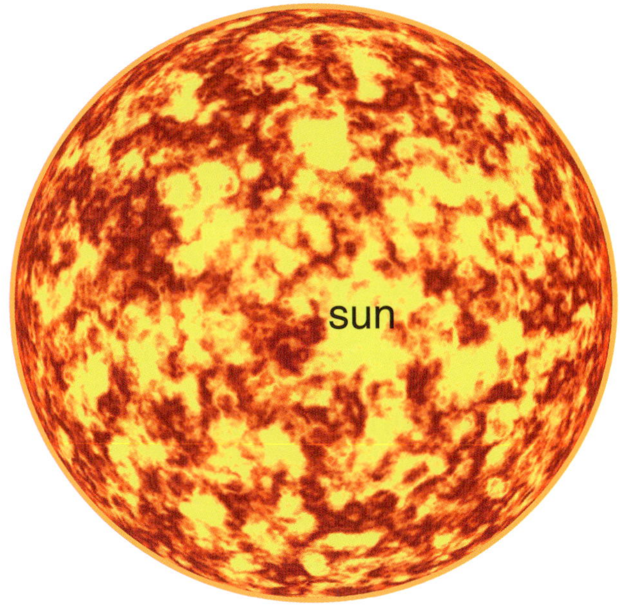

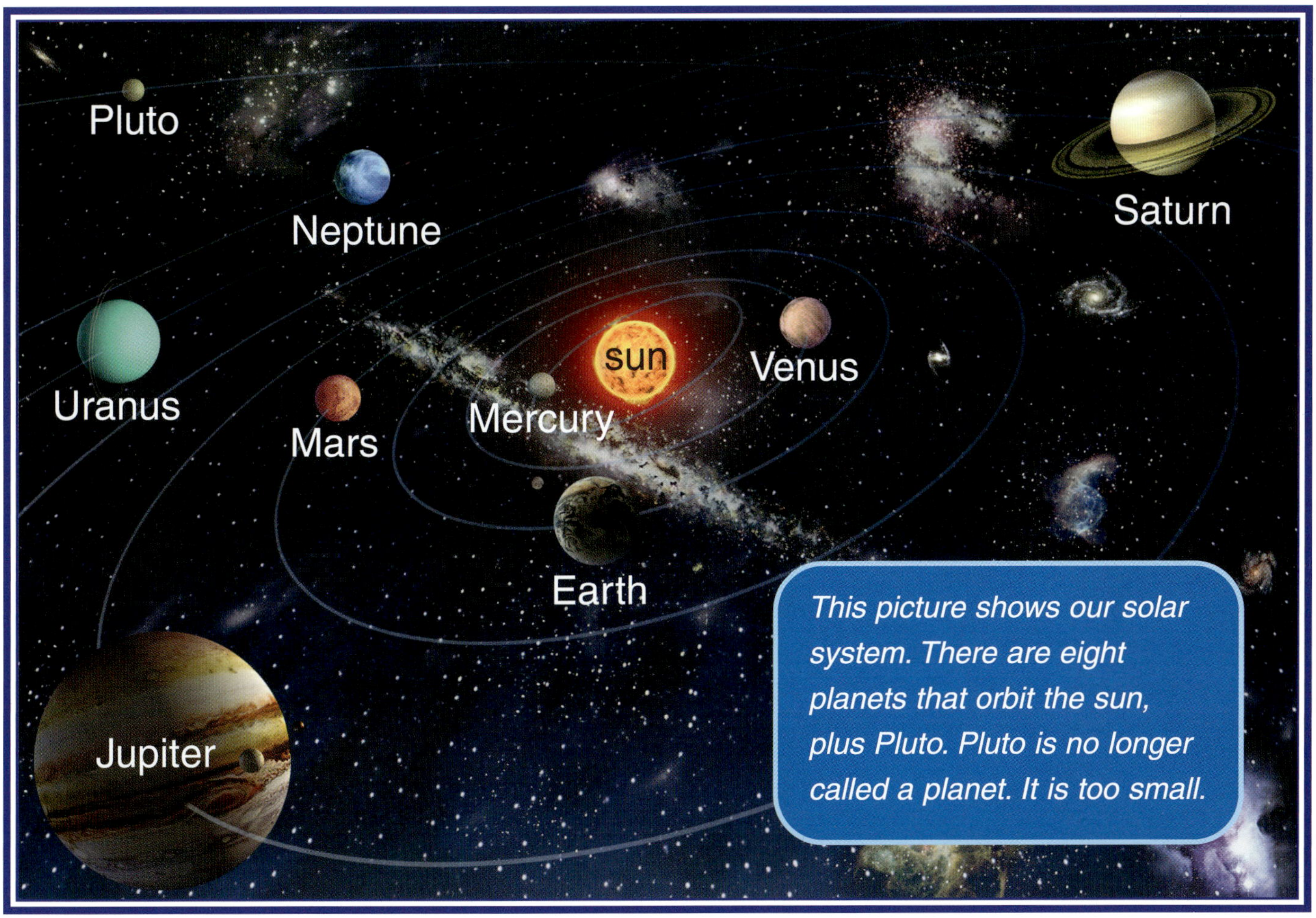

This picture shows our solar system. There are eight planets that orbit the sun, plus Pluto. Pluto is no longer called a planet. It is too small.

Day and night

As Earth travels around the sun, it slowly turns in circles. It takes one day for Earth to turn in a full circle. For about half of the day, the part of Earth where you live faces the sun. When Earth faces the sun, it is daylight in your part of the world. For the other half of the day, the part of Earth where you live faces away from the sun. When Earth faces away from the sun, it is nighttime in your part of the world.

During the day, you can see the sun in the sky.

Night, day, night, day

Each day has a nighttime and a daytime. Night follows day, and day follows night. When something repeats, there is a **pattern**. How many times does the night-and-day pattern repeat in a week?

At night, you can see the moon in the sky above.

During the day, there is a lot of light. The sun lights the Earth.

At night, the sun does not light the Earth. You have to turn on lights so you can see.

Hot and cold

Not all parts of Earth get the same amount of sunlight. Areas near the **North Pole** and the **South Pole** never get a lot of sunlight. The North Pole is at the top of Earth. The South Pole is at the bottom of Earth. These parts of Earth are always cold.

The North Pole is cold and snowy. Polar bears live there.

Ice and snow cover the South Pole. Penguins live there.

Hot and sunny

The middle part of Earth is called the **equator**. The equator gets a lot of sunlight all year. The area near the equator is always very hot and sunny.

*When the sun rises and **sets**, or goes down, it is low in the sky. This picture shows a sunset. The sun will soon be gone, and it will be nighttime.*

The four seasons

There is a big area on Earth between the North Pole and the equator. There is also a big area between the South Pole and the equator. These areas are not always hot or cold. They have four **seasons**. The seasons are spring, summer, autumn, and winter. A season is a period of time that has certain weather and **temperatures**. Temperature measures how hot or cold something is.

In spring, the weather is warm and rainy. Flowers bloom, and baby animals are born.

Summer days are hot and sunny. Children have fun swimming!

In autumn, the weather is cool and cloudy. Leaves fall off the trees. Winter is coming soon!

Winter days are cold. Children wear warm clothes. In some places, they play in the snow.

A tilted planet

Earth is **tilted**. When something is tilted, it is not straight up and down. As Earth travels around the sun, different parts of Earth are tilted toward the sun at different times. The tilt of the Earth causes the seasons to change.

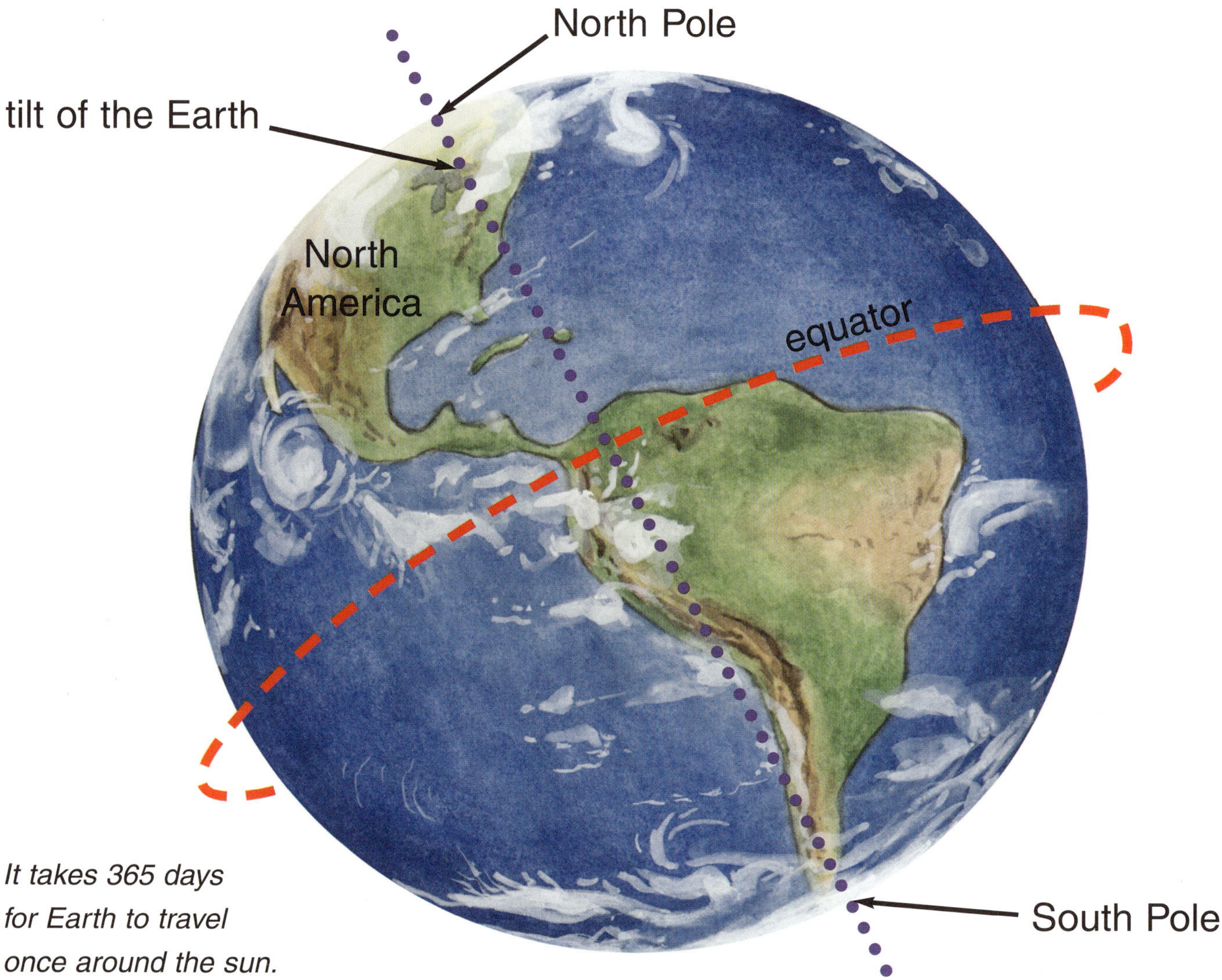

It takes 365 days for Earth to travel once around the sun.

More or less light and heat

Each season gets a different amount of sunlight. Each season also gets a different amount of heat from the sun. The light and heat from the sun change the temperatures of the seasons. This diagram shows the seasons in North America.

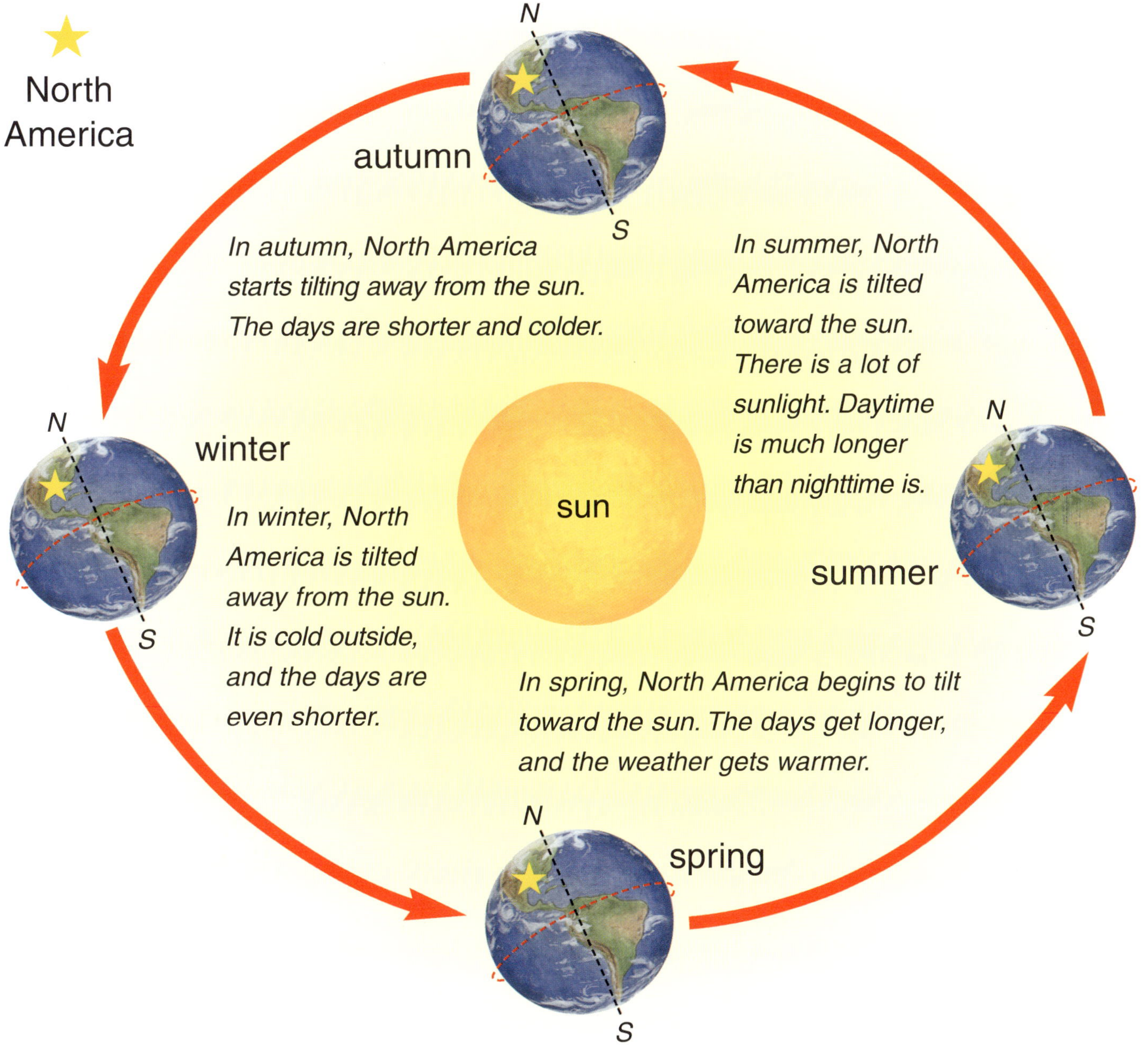

Food from sunlight

Many plants grow in spring and summer. The weather is warm, and there is plenty of sunlight. Plants use sunlight to make their own food! Using sunlight to make food is called **photosynthesis**. Plants take in sunlight through a green color in their leaves or stems. The green color is called **chlorophyll**.

Chlorophyll gives these leaves their green color.

Air and water

Plants use air and water to make food from sunlight. Plants take in air through tiny holes in their leaves. They take in water through their **roots**. Roots are the underground parts of plants.

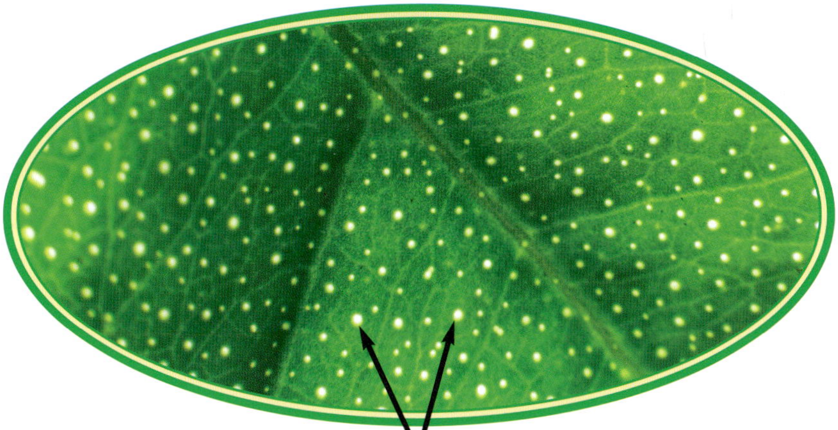

*Plants breathe through small holes in their leaves called **stomata**.*

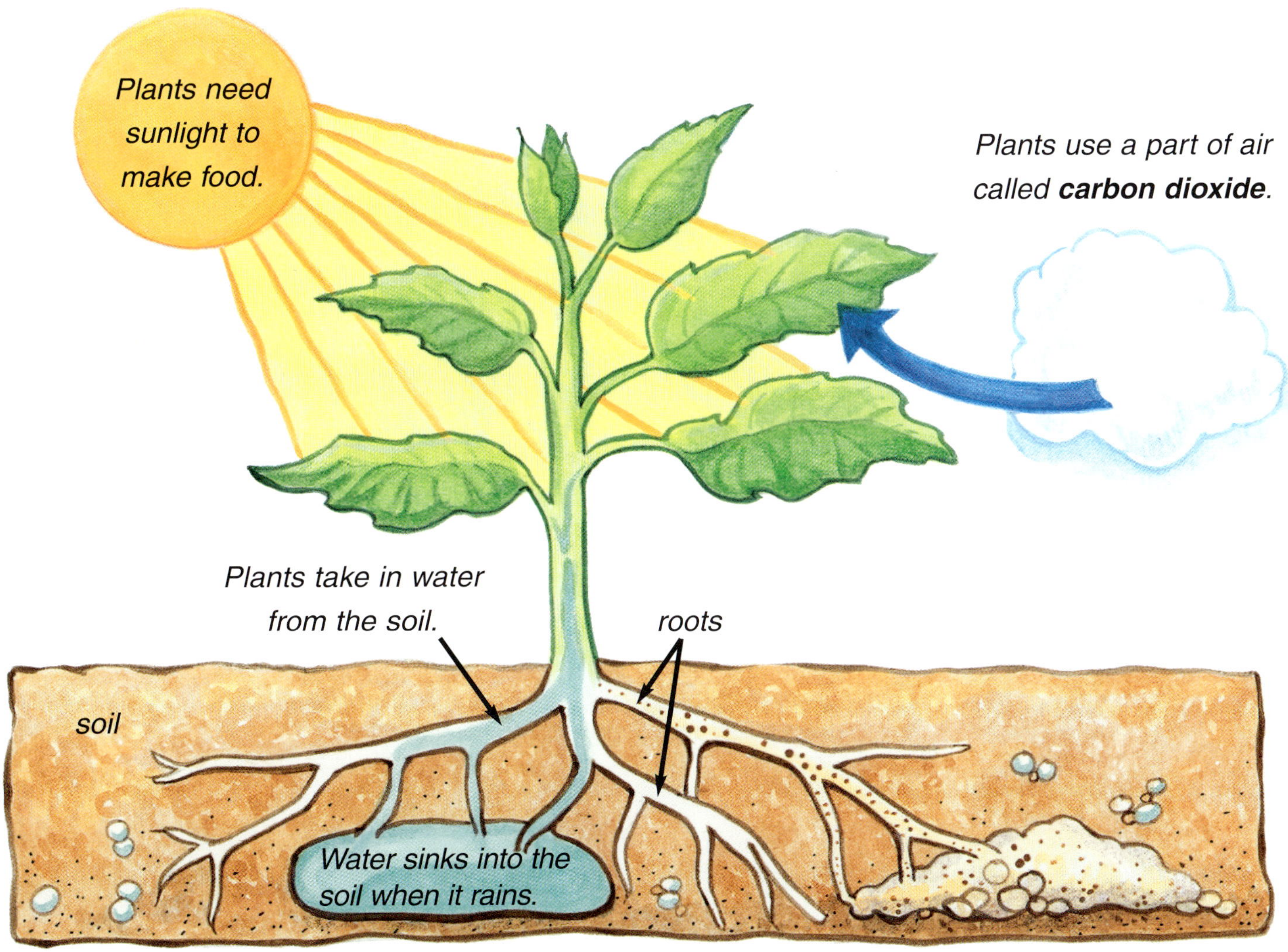

Less sunshine

Plants look different in different seasons. Trees have bright green leaves in spring and summer. In autumn, the leaves of trees are red, orange, or yellow. Why do the leaves change color?

Green makes food

The leaves of trees change color because of the sun! In spring and summer, the sun shines for many hours each day. Trees can make a lot of food in their leaves. They use chlorophyll, their green color, to make the food.

Losing the green

In autumn, there are fewer hours of sunlight each day. Trees cannot make as much food. Without food, the green color in the leaves fades. The red and yellow colors in the leaves show through.

The green color in this leaf is fading. Other colors are showing through.

Without food, leaves die by the end of autumn. When the leaves die, they fall off the trees. Most trees do not have leaves in winter.

Go to sleep or fly away?

The lives of animals also change when there is less sunlight. In winter, the days are short and dark. It is cold outside. Some animals cannot keep warm. These animals sleep through most of the winter. Before they go to sleep, the animals gather food. Some animals also gather soft grasses and leaves to make warm beds.

This squirrel will sleep through most of the winter. Before it goes to sleep, it will gather food and store it in or near its home. The squirrel will wake up during the winter and eat some of the food.

Warmer places

Some animals do not sleep through winter. They **migrate**, or move, to warmer places with more sunshine. Many birds fly south in autumn. They return home in the spring.

flying to warmer places

Shorter days

Sunlight tells animals when to prepare for sleep or when to leave their homes. In autumn, the days slowly start getting shorter. When days get shorter, they also get colder. Shorter, colder days tell animals that winter is coming!

flying home

Canada geese fly away for the winter. They return home in the spring to have babies.

What are shadows?

On a bright sunny day, you can see many **shadows**. Shadows are dark areas. They are made by blocking light. Shadows have the same shapes as the things that block the light. This girl is blocking sunlight from reaching the ground. Her body makes a shadow. The shadow is almost the same shape as the shape of the girl's body.

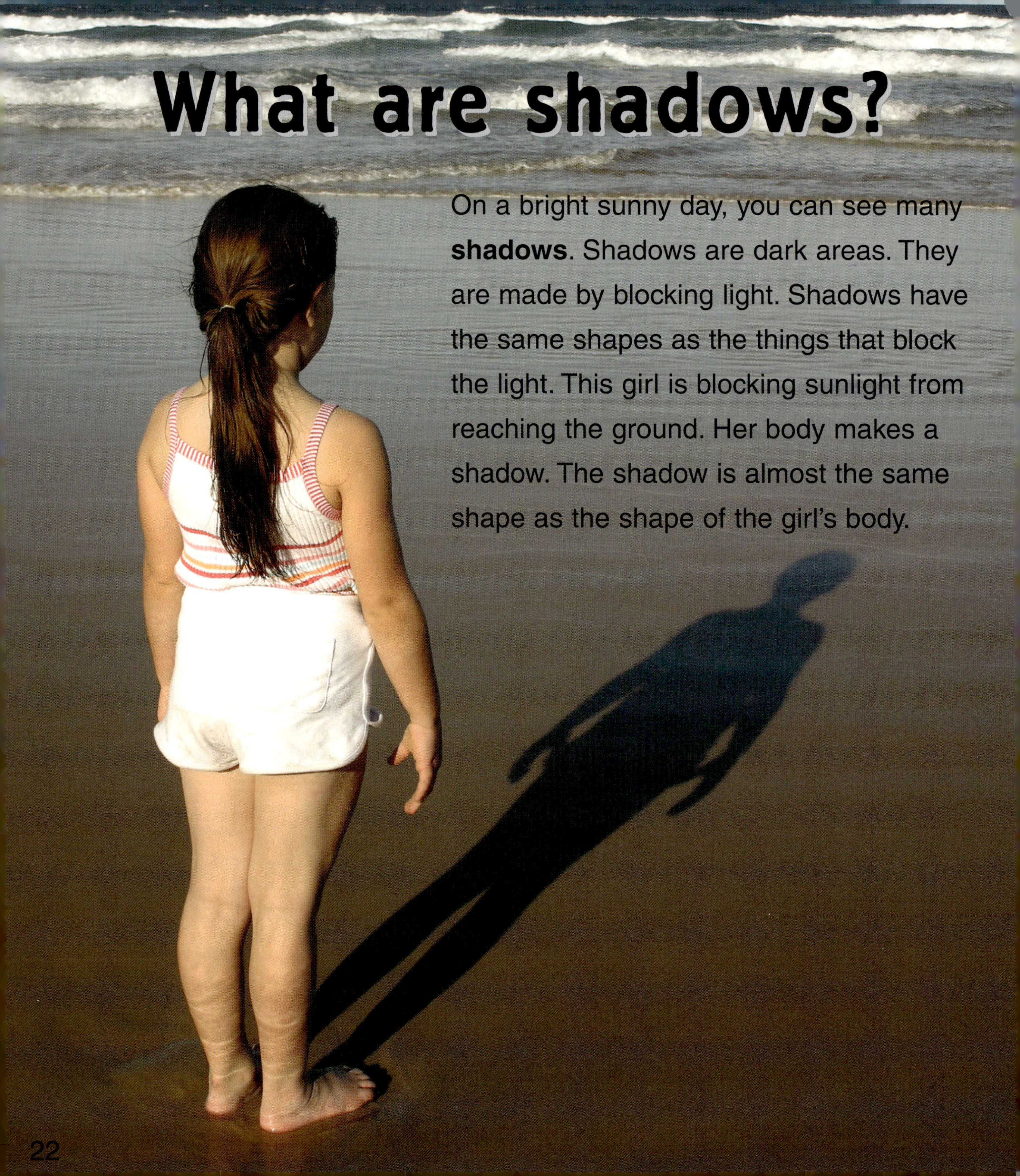

Changing shadows

As Earth turns slowly each day, the sun appears in different places in the sky. At noon, the sun is right over your head. In the morning and afternoon, the sun seems to be lower in the sky. As the sun's position changes, the shadows that it makes also change.

(right) When the sun is high in the sky, it makes short shadows.

When the sun is lower in the sky, the shadows are much longer. The shadow of this boy and his bicycle is bigger than the boy and the bike.

Mirror, mirror

Mirrors, windows, and other shiny objects have smooth **surfaces**. When sunlight shines on an object near a smooth surface, it does not create a shadow. It creates a **reflection**. A reflection is an image that looks like the object near the shiny surface. A reflection in a mirror looks just like the object that is close to the mirror.

This girl's face is next to a mirror. Which is the girl, and which is the reflection of the girl? How can you tell?

Water also makes reflections. How is the reflection of these buildings different from the reflection of the girl who is jumping above the water?

How would this girl's reflection look if the water below her were still?

There is not enough sunlight to see this boy's face, the color of his clothing, or his reflection. There is only a ***silhouette*** *of the boy. A silhouette is a dark shape and an outline of a person or an object.*

Changing water

Water is always changing. Water changes when it is heated and cooled by the sun. Water can be **liquid**, **solid**, or **vapor**. Liquid water has no shape. It flows. Ice and snow are solid water. They have shapes. Vapor is water that is part of air. It floats above the ground. Water vapor is in the air all around you.

Liquid water flows in oceans, rivers, and lakes. When liquid water gets very cold, it freezes and turns to ice. Ice is solid water. When the sun heats ice, ice melts and becomes liquid water again. Is this polar bear standing on solid or liquid water?

Water vapor

At night, there is no sunlight. The water in oceans and lakes cools. When the sun rises in the morning, the heat of the sun warms the top part of the water. This heated water turns to vapor and becomes part of the air. When the wind lifts the water vapor high into the sky, clouds form.

*Water vapor that is close to the ground is called **mist** or **fog**. Fog is thicker than mist. It is hard to see through fog.*

Colors of sunlight

Sunlight gives us colors. You can see the colors of the sun in **rainbows**. Rainbows are curves of colored light in the sky. Rainbows form when sunlight shines through tiny drops of water in the air. You can see rainbows in the sky over water. You can also see rainbows over land after it rains.

Colors of the rainbow

There are seven colors in a rainbow. They are always in the same order. The colors are red, orange, yellow, green, blue, **indigo**, and violet. Indigo is a dark purple-blue color. Every color you see is made up of these colors.

The sun gives us all the beautiful colors on Earth. Which colors do you see in this girl's flower wreath? Which rainbow colors are missing?

The sun's energy

All **energy** comes from the sun. Energy is the power that living things need to move, grow, and change. Plants use the energy of the sun to make food. The sun's energy then becomes part of plants. Some animals get the sun's energy by eating plants. Animals that eat mainly plants are called **herbivores**.

A food chain

Some animals eat other animals. Animals that eat mainly other animals are called **carnivores**. Lions are carnivores. They eat antelopes. Antelopes eat plants. They get the sun's energy from the plants they eat. Lions get the sun's energy when they eat antelopes. Both animals get the sun's energy from the food they eat. When the energy of the sun is passed from a plant to an animal and then to another animal, there is a **food chain**.

How do we get energy?

People also get the sun's energy from the foods we eat. Most people are **omnivores**. Omnivores eat plant foods and meat. Meat comes from animals. Cheese, milk, and eggs come from animals, as well. Vegetables and fruits are parts of plants. Foods such as noodles, rice, and bread come from **grains**. Grains are the seeds of plants such as wheat. Name three plant foods that these children are eating.

This burger contains two animal foods and three plant foods. Which are the animal foods? Which are the plant foods?

Words to know

carnivore An animal that eats other animals

chlorophyll A green color found in plants that takes in sunlight and helps plants make food

energy The power living things get from food, which helps them move and grow

fog Thick water vapor that is near the ground

food chain A pattern of eating and being eaten; for example, a plant is eaten by an antelope, which is then eaten by a lion

grain The seed of a plant such as wheat

herbivore An animal that eats mainly plants

migrate To move from one place to another to find warmer weather

mist Fine water vapor that is near the ground

omnivore A person or animal that eats both plants and animals

photosynthesis The use of sunlight by plants in making food from air and water

planet A large object that moves in circles around a star and does not make its own light

reflection An image that is seen on a shiny surface, which looks like a nearby object

shadow A dark area made by blocking light

solar system The planets, their moons, and other objects that travel around the sun

surface The top or outside layer of an object

Index